# RIGHT IS WRONG

# RIGHT IS WRONG

*The Case against Conservatism*

STEPHEN SCHADE

iUniverse, Inc.
Bloomington

# Right Is Wrong
## The Case against Conservatism

iUniverse books may be ordered through booksellers or by contacting:

iUniverse
1663 Liberty Drive
Bloomington, IN 47403
www.iuniverse.com
1-800-Authors (1-800-288-4677)

ISBN: 978-1-4759-4662-8 (sc)
ISBN: 978-1-4759-4664-2 (e)

Library of Congress Control Number: 2012916327

Printed in the United States of America

iUniverse rev. date: 12/10/2012

# CONTENTS

# List of Tables

# LIST OF PICTURES

# PREFACE

**B**ecause my father was staunchly Republican, producing a book like this one may seem puzzling to some. Perhaps it was because I was a child of the '60s. Or maybe it was due to the logical approach to problem solving that I received in my science and engineering courses. Whatever the reason, I began to stray from the conservative fold in high school with my opposition to the Vietnam War. By college, I had already become an independent, and then I was decidedly liberal as an adult. As I contemplated this transition, I wondered whether there were inherent characteristics that made one perspective better than the other. Thus followed over twenty years of research, culminating in the publication of this book. Ironically, my father deserves some credit for this, as I inherited his strong interest in politics.

I am writing this in the hope that others will follow the same journey. Some make the switch because of single issues. For example, the Brady family became gun control supporters because of a family tragedy.[1] And Montana has moved toward the Democratic column because of the high rate of health problems experienced by miners in that state.[2] However, by moving away from single issues and focusing instead on the core values of the liberal and conservative philosophies, I hope that those who have not experienced a life-changing event will also consider the merits of changing their views.

# Introduction

Most discussions on politics are about issues—gun control or health care, for example. Rarely do we discuss the merits of liberalism or conservatism themselves. My book, *Right Is Wrong: The Case against Conservatism*, is unique in this regard. Basically, it takes a look at liberalism and conservatism from political, social, historical, and economic perspectives and then draws conclusions. It builds on the observations by historians that politics in this country moves in thirty-year cycles, looks at events in each cycle, and analyzes their impact.

This book reflects a long journey. Having been raised by a die-hard Republican father, writing a book like this one may seem mystifying to some. But as only Nixon can go to China, so only a convert can make a convincing argument. As I considered my switch to liberalism, I wondered whether there were intrinsic attributes that made one philosophy superior to the other. The research that followed resulted in this book.

After examining the tide of history, the book looks at the personal side of one's beliefs. It shows how being liberal or conservative can influence the choices we make in our lives. Then it illustrates how choices based on each view also affect the business world. One chapter discusses the dark side of conservatism. It shows how it affects society and influences individual behavior, often in negative ways. Finally, the book outlines a path forward for the readers. Those who accept the facts and conclusions are invited on a journey to liberalism.

# Chapter 1
# The Big Debate

"Don't discuss politics or religion." How often have we heard that line? Yet we ignore it all the time, usually without starting a war. However, most of our discussions are about issues—tax policy or foreign affairs, for instance. Rarely does anyone debate the merits of conservatism or liberalism themselves. Is there really an advantage to either view?

Historians have found that society tends to swing from one position to the other every thirty years or so.[3] Based on this observation, it might seem that there is no clear advantage to either one. A closer look at major social, economic, and political events in each era shows a trend, however. While the exact dates are subject to debate, the overall pattern is clear. Social changes that have lasted all occurred during the liberal periods. On the other hand, those made in conservative times were all discarded.

## Periods in American History
## Conservative vs. Liberal

1903–1918 (Liberal)

Conservation

NAACP

Boy Scouts, Girl Scouts,
   Campfire Girls

National Collegiate
   Athletic Association

Federal Reserve System

Rotary Club

Pure Food and Drug Act

1918–1933 (Conservative)

Prohibition

Antitrust

Margin buying

1933–1948 (Liberal)

Social Security

National Labor Relations Act

Elimination of gold standard

Minimum wage

Alcoholics Anonymous

1948–1963 (Conservative)

McCarthyism

1963–1978 (Liberal)

Environmentalism

Civil rights

Women's rights

Medicare

Voting rights


1978–1993 (Conservative)

Supply-side economics

Junk bonds


1993–2008 (Liberal)

Gay rights/partnerships

Death penalty reform

Medicare drug reform

Medical marijuana

Brady gun law

Education/school funding reform


Skeptics will undoubtedly point to the exception to shoot down this argument, which is that school desegregation occurred during the 1950s. However, all Supreme Court justices but one were holdovers from the long Democratic reign, so the court ended up being out of step with the rest of society. And opposing arguments ignore the fundamental conclusion that liberal changes become ingrained in society.

Nor does a president's party indicate whether the prevailing tide is liberal or conservative. Nixon was elected because the

Democrats miscalculated on Vietnam,[4] yet he signed off on Title IX[5] (equality for women in sports) and environmental legislation.[6] Bush 43 won primarily because of problems with the butterfly ballot in Palm Beach County, Florida.[7] During his term, we got Medicare D (prescription drug benefit)[8] and education reform.[9] Accidents of history sometimes make strange bedfellows.

Some would claim that we were in a conservative era since Reagan and it only ended with Obama's election. Events listed in the table suggest otherwise, however. Moreover, if Obama ushered in a liberal era, the Blue Dogs (conservative Democrats) would have been out of favor, and we would have gotten nationalized health care.[10] In reality, the nation was making a turn toward another conservative period.

# Chapter 2
# The Tide of History

A look at history shows the relative performance of liberalism and conservatism. The difference pervades all of society, not just politics.

*Politics*

When President Clinton was asked to name his greatest mistake, he said it was not sending soldiers to Rwanda to stop the genocide.[11] George W. Bush's response to the same question listed nothing during his presidency. He would only admit that trading Sammy Sosa when he was president of the Texas Rangers was a mistake.[12] Even Robert McNamara finally admitted that Vietnam was ill-advised.[13] Yet, to the end, Nixon maintained, "I am not a crook."[14] A liberal perspective, it seems, allows us to face our faults. Conservatives, whose Eleventh Commandment will not allow them to criticize a fellow Republican,[15] will not even point the finger at themselves. They would have you believe that they are always right.

One test of the strength of one's beliefs is a willingness to sacrifice. In the political realm, this involves giving up votes to do what one believes is the right thing to do and is in the best interest of the country. Democrats have lost votes on numerous occasions in implementing their agenda. They lost the endorsement of organized labor for a number of subsequent elections after Bobby Kennedy went after Jimmy Hoffa.[16] As Lyndon Johnson predicted, they lost the South over civil rights. More recently, they gave up their longtime control of the House by passing gun control legislation (in 1994).[17]

Republicans, on the other hand, trade beliefs for votes. Since Reagan, they have given up their long-held belief that balanced budgets matter. When asked about this, Republican strategists point out that fiscal responsibility is far down on the priority list of most voters. They believe their position will not cost them votes.[18] In an ironic twist, Democrats most recently have championed balanced budgets.

Another example of Republican priorities is the dividend tax. They wanted to end the double taxation of dividends since it was imposed on both corporations and individuals. Many economists believe that eliminating the tax on companies would be more beneficial to the economy because most dividends paid to individuals go to accounts that are already tax sheltered.[19] But companies do not vote, of course, so the tax was instead lowered on individuals.

*Economics*

Ten of the last eleven major recessions have occurred during Republican administrations.[20] Some in the GOP (Grand Old

Party, another name for the Republican Party) will argue that the downturns were actually caused by Democrats and they were left to clean up the mess.[21] A closer look shows a number of problems with this view. First of all, in seven of the cases, the recessions started so deep into Republican control of the White House (Hoover, Eisenhower [the last two], Nixon, Ford, Bush 41, and the second one under Bush 43) that they could not plausibly be blamed on Democrats. Both gross domestic product (GDP) and industrial production grew at faster rates under Truman than under Eisenhower,[22] so it is unrealistic to blame Truman for the early 1950s recession. Because job growth under Carter was greater than under Reagan,[23] it is unreasonable to say Carter caused the early 1980s recession. (Many economists blame the Fed, or Federal Reserve System).[24] Finally, the first downturn of Bush 43's presidency was caused not by a president but by a Republican Fed chairman, Alan Greenspan.

At this point, a closer look at Greenspan's record is in order because he probably caused more damage to America than any other person in history. Two former Republican presidents, Ford and Bush 41, criticized him for responding too slowly to conditions during their terms.[25] Greenspan also championed the big bang theory of instantly converting from communism to capitalism that devastated Russia's economy in the 1990s.[26] He caused the first recession under Bush 43 by raising interest rates even though no inflation was in sight.[27] Enron went down because of derivatives that had his support.[28] And the second Bush 43 recession began because he drove interest rates so low that it became too easy to borrow money.[29] All the while, he insisted that the free market would prevent the ensuing meltdown.[30] He indeed has a sad record.

Nixon's Fed appointees, who raised interest rates in a failed effort to stem inflation, caused both recessions in the 1970s.[31] Nixon's own wage and price controls exacerbated both of them. But two factors that were beyond the Fed's control caused inflation:

- Energy prices surged because of the Arab oil embargo and the Iranian revolution.
- The influx of the large baby boom generation into the housing market caused home prices and rents to soar. People bought houses regardless of the interest rate because they could always refinance once rates went down.

Inflation finally subsided in the early 1980s when Organization of Petroleum Exporting Countries (OPEC) members began to cheat on their quotas[32] and the boomers' home-buying spree ended. The Fed needs to better discern when an interest rate policy cannot affect inflationary causes. Otherwise, they will end up causing recessions, which goes against their goal of creating a strong economy. The Fed put the "stag" in "stagflation" (stagnation + inflation).

Those in the GOP who do not blame these recessions on Democrats will instead claim that the economy has been better under Democrats because they start wars and run budget deficits to boost the economy.[33] Prior to Clinton, there appeared to be a cause-and-effect relationship here. Certainly, the economy boomed during the wars of the 1940s and 1960s. However, Clinton ushered in the greatest expansion in American history during a period of peace, and he balanced the budget for the first time in three decades.[34]

Why then is the economy better under the Democrats? Primarily, they are willing to regulate the markets. That conclusion became obvious at the end of Bush 43's term when massive deficits and two wars failed to prevent the worst recession since the Great Depression. Margin buying precipitated the latter. In the late 1980s, the collapse of the junk-bond market hurt the economy. And, of course, the late 2000s downturn was caused when the Securities and Exchange Commission (SEC) lifted the net capital rule that limited banks to loaning a specified multiple of their assets.[35] By setting standards, Democrats assure that the worst excesses of the market are not realized.

Along with gross domestic product (GDP), the stock market performs better under Democratic presidents. From 1929 through 1995, the S&P 500 index averaged 14 percent a year under Democrats but only 6 percent annually during GOP administrations.[36] Some claim that the stock market is best in periods of divided government, that is, when Democrats control the White House and Republicans dominate Congress. This view has a couple of problems:

- The opposite is not also true. The market does not do as well when Republicans have the presidency while Democrats run Congress.[37]
- Data suggesting that conclusion is misleading because Congress determines fiscal, not economic, policy. The chairmen of the Fed and the SEC, along with the secretary of the treasury, are very powerful people who greatly influence our lives. Their roles became much clearer during the 2000s debacle and the subsequent bailout plan.[38]

Some analysts will use the years before 1929 to show that Democrats hold only a slim advantage in stock market growth. True, the bulls stampeded under Coolidge.[39] However, unregulated margin buying created that bubble. It finally burst, just as the housing market did in the 2000s. So, only years encompassing current margin regulations are used to make a valid comparison.

Another reason that earlier years do not allow a good comparison is that the two parties have changed places over the past hundred years. At one time, the party of Lincoln stood for helping the oppressed. It began to stray from that view for the same reason that Teddy Roosevelt, a conservationist, left the Republican Party. It became too cozy with big business.[40] Big business has never treated workers well, and they fight environmental laws every step of the way. Northeasterners figured that out a few decades ago and made the switch from red to blue. More recently, the Midwestern states have become Democratic.[41] Now, some Western states are making the same transition. If Abe and Teddy were alive today, they would be Democrats.

Perhaps the best thing the Democrats did to help the economy in the long term was the elimination of the gold standard in the 1930s. After this change, both the length and frequency of recessions decreased.[42] That is why the Great Depression has not repeated itself. A flexible currency can more quickly respond to prevailing conditions.

*Sociology*

Social trends also reflect the times. Loud colors and new styles tend to dominate the liberal eras. However, the changes run deeper than this. Most civic organizations were started during the first liberal period of the twentieth century, as people recognized the need to help others. The National Collegiate Athletic Association (NCAA), which still governs college sports, was established to reduce the serious injuries then prevalent in college football. Alcoholics Anonymous (AA) was created during the second liberal time frame in recognition of that fact that those people could be helped.

During the last liberal period, business casual began to dominate the workplace. This trend even spilled over into places of worship, as people realized they did not have to dress up to show respect to God. And the majority of the public finally became supportive of gay rights.

Conservative trends reflect the times but then fizzle out. Unregulated margin buying, McCarthyism, and junk bonds ended up in the dustbin of history. Progress always wins out in the end.

*Science*

Some anecdotal evidence also suggests that the innovative spirit of liberalism fosters scientific progress. This trend seems particularly prominent in the field of medicine.

By the time my mother died of multiple myeloma, a rare cancer, in 1995, I had done much research on the subject. The drugs used to treat her were developed in the 1960s. A few years after her death, I read of a couple of breakthroughs. One involved thalidomide, a drug that had fallen into disrepute in the 1960s because it caused birth defects after being given to pregnant women to treat morning sickness. However, it showed promise in curing multiple myeloma and was given to former vice presidential candidate Geraldine Ferraro for that purpose. Stem cell transplants also showed benefits in treating this disease.

When my cousin developed multiple sclerosis in the 1980s, there was little the doctors could do for her. She ended up in a wheelchair. Then, in the 1990s, researchers discovered that beta interferon countered the effects of the gamma interferon that appeared in the spinal fluid during flare-ups. After she started taking beta interferon, her condition improved, and she is no longer in a wheelchair. Looking at the big picture shows a similar trend. Antibiotic sulfa drugs were developed in the 1930s, measles and Sabin oral vaccines came along in the 1960s, and the human genome was mapped in the 1990s.

This phenomenon does not seem to be exhibited in the other fields of science. Perhaps that is because scientists usually do not interact with the public. As a result, they are isolated from prevailing social trends. Medical professionals, on the other hand, do make contact with the general population and are probably more likely to reflect what is going on around them. Another possible explanation is that scientists, like university professors, are a decidedly liberal lot, and there is also data to support this conclusion.[43]

*Culture*

Liberal periods tend to foster the arts as well. Most comic book heroes were created during the liberal times outlined in chapter 1, as the following list illustrates:[44]

Dick Tracy (1931)

Superman (1938)

Batman (1939)

Wonder Woman (1941)

Spider-Man (1962)

The Hulk (1962)

The X-Men (1963)

Most of our modern Christmas songs also originated in a flurry that began in the 1930s:[45]

"Santa Claus Is Comin' to Town" (1932)

"I Wonder as I Wander" (1933)

"Winter Wonderland" (1934)

"Carol of the Bells" (1936)

"The Little Drummer Boy" (1941)

"Happy Holiday" (1942)

"White Christmas" (1942)

"I'll Be Home for Christmas" (1943)

"Have Yourself a Merry Little Christmas" (1944)

"Let It Snow! Let It Snow! Let It Snow!" (1945)

"All I Want for Christmas Is My Two Front Teeth" (1946)

"Here Comes Santa Claus" (1946)

"The Christmas Song" (1946)

"Sleigh Ride" (1948/1950)

"A Marshmallow World" (1949)

"Rudolph the Red-Nosed Reindeer" (1949)

"Frosty the Snowman" (1950)

"Silver Bells" (1951)

"It's Beginning to Look a Lot Like Christmas" (1951)

The years above do not exactly agree with those in chapter 1. That shows the difficulty in assigning precise dates to liberal and conservative cycles or to any historical periods, for that matter. For example, historians generally use the year 1750 as the dividing line between the Baroque and Classical periods of classical music. Of course, some composers in the middle of the eighteenth century exhibited elements of both styles. Nevertheless, few would disagree that the Golden Age of rock music occurred during the 1960s and early 1970s. And alternative rock rose to prominence in the 1990s. Most importantly, though, it is the overall trend that is instructive, not the specific dates.

## Fashion

Clothing styles tend to be more colorful and innovative during liberal periods. Conservative times, on the other hand, involve a return to the past. Only natural fabrics—wool, cotton, and silk—are used,[46] and there are far fewer no-iron garments available. It seems that conservatives would either have us devote more time to ironing or live with more wrinkles in our clothes.

Women's hemlines also tend to rise during liberal times (also during the conservative 1920s). Of course, as previously discussed, the stock market tends to do better during liberal eras. These trends support the observation that the market parallels the rise and fall of skirt lengths.

Photograph ©Raimond Spekking/CC-BY-SA-3.0
(via Wikimedia Commons)

# Chapter 3
# The Personal Side

N ot only do liberalism and conservatism affect the economy and national issues, they also determine the choices we make in everyday life.

*Investing*

How people invest money also depends on whether they are conservative or liberal. Conservatives prefer certificates of deposit (CDs) and money market funds, which are safer asset classes (uncertainty avoidance, loss prevention).[47] Liberals are more willing to buy stocks, which are riskier but have better returns (uncertainty tolerance).[48] My former employer provided a good example. It was revealed that 86 percent of the 401(k) money was invested in the capital preservation fund, with only 14 percent in stocks. The workforce was heavily male and leaned strongly to the right politically.

## Ethics

One's political persuasion also shapes personal ethics. This is particularly true in admitting mistakes. As previously mentioned, Bill Clinton and Robert McNamara were willing to admit mistakes, while George W. Bush and Richard Nixon were not. And no one in the Reagan administration has ever admitted that supply-side economics was a misstep that started us down the road of massive budget deficits. While neither party can claim perfection, at least Democrats are more willing to go on the record about it.

## Complex Decisions

Conservatives generally believe that issues are black and white. They do not acknowledge the many facets of an argument or the gray areas in between. Consequently, they have difficulty with complex decisions (intolerance of ambiguity).[49] That explains why they are not as good at leadership positions, as will be discussed later.

## Optimism

Studies show that conservatives have more nightmares than liberals.[50] In particular, they had more nightmares and dreams in which they lacked power. Liberals, on the other hand, had a greater frequency of good fortune in their dreams. This indicated a greater sense of optimism. Even when we sleep, our beliefs affect us.

## Social

Political views affect our social relationships. This is especially true when it comes to divorce. A look at divorce statistics shows that the highest rate is in the South, the most conservative region of America.[51] Ironically, the Bible Belt is the Divorce Belt. Some have tried to find other reasons to explain this trend. For example, they point to the higher proportion of Catholics, whose church takes a strong position against divorce, in the Northeast. However, the divorce rate is nearly identical among Catholics and Protestants.[52] Another possible proposed explanation is income disparity. Because the cost of living varies throughout the country, however, it is not possible to make a fair comparison using income. A better measure is poverty rate. Oklahoma, Alabama, Arkansas, and Tennessee all have similar poverty rates,[53] with divorce rates about 50 percent above the national average. Yet New York, with a nearly identical poverty rate, has a divorce rate that is well below the national average.

Clearly, the only plausible explanation for this difference in regional divorce rates is political viewpoint. This should really come as no surprise. After all, one trait of liberalism is open-mindedness, so liberals are more willing to forgive mistakes and see another person's point of view. This open-mindedness is a quality that makes strong relationships. It also explains why college graduates, trained to be open-minded in evaluating situations, are less likely to get divorced[54] and more likely to vote Democratic.[55]

***

Unfortunately, conservatives often see a different perspective only when they have actually been in a particular situation. Dick Cheney, for instance, supports same-sex marriage because his daughter is a lesbian,[56] but he also approves of torture.[57] John McCain, on the other hand, opposes torture due to his time as a prisoner of war in Vietnam,[58] but he is against gay marriage.[59] It is important to understand that all people have valid concerns as a result of their experiences in life.

# Chapter 4
# Mind Your Business

*Leaders*

Research shows that companies with liberal chief executive officers (CEOs) are more profitable than those run by conservatives. That conclusion is not surprising because liberals tend to be more innovative (scientists are overwhelmingly liberal) and treat their employees better. Also, as previously discussed, they are better at complex decision making. For all these reasons, liberals make not only better CEOs but also better presidents. That George W. Bush failed as a president after running oil companies that never enjoyed great success[60] and presiding over a mediocre Texas Rangers team that never made the playoffs[61] should not have been unexpected.

A corollary to this study is a finding that women make better managers than men.[62] This result could be predicted based on the fact that female voters are more liberal, the so-called "gender gap."

One conservative view is that layoffs make a company more competitive. Yet research shows that staff reductions during the early 1990s recession failed to improve profitability during the subsequent recovery about 70 percent of the time.[63] And this was during the greatest economic expansion in American history. So employees paid the price for the mistakes of management.

Republicans claim to be the party that is friendly to big business. They say that Democratic rules and regulations stifle business. As previously seen, however, the economy performs better under Democratic presidents. Innovation, not fewer rules, is the key to making a company more profitable.

## Design

Companies that adopt innovative technology, even if they are among the first to do so, generally perform better. By doing so, they cut costs and gain market share.

Companies that maintain the status quo believe they can continue to make profits by doing what they have always done. Unfortunately, they often get passed by. General Motors is a prime example of this mind-set. In the late 1950s and early 1960s, an influx of smaller, more fuel-efficient cars cut into the market share for American automobile companies. They fought back, however, and regained their dominance. Once they had done so, they fell back into their old ways. As a result, market share once again began to erode. General Motors, being the most conservative of the American companies, suffered the most.[64] In the end, the late 2000s recession forced them into bankruptcy.

# Chapter 5
# The Dark Side

P eople tend to think that being conservative is just a matter of preference. They believe that, while this choice makes them different from liberals, they are otherwise well-adjusted people. However, conservatism has a dark side, both in how it affects society and how it influences individual behavior.

*Law of Unintended Consequences*
Whenever liberals propose a change, one conservative criticism is to cite the Law of Unintended Consequences as a reason not to pursue it. If we cannot predict the outcome, we should not try it, their argument goes. What they need to do, of course, is apply this principle to their own programs. Supply-side economics led to huge budget deficits. Savings and loan deregulation destroyed many of those institutions.[65] And elimination of the net capital rule, which limits bank lending, led to subprime loans and a financial meltdown. If conservatives really took this belief to

heart, they would look in the mirror and practice what they preach.

## *Mental Attitude*

Conservatism has some characteristics that influence mental attitude. This is a strong statement, but the facts tend to support it.

One characteristic of a conservative view is being out of touch with reality. How can one be more out of touch with reality than by living in the past, in a world that no longer exists? This approach is exhibited by conservatives who oppose scientific discoveries, such as global warming. Another feature of conservatism is repeating the same behavior and expecting different results. Who exemplifies that more than those who believe the old way is always best? Such people are extremely resistant to change. They admit, for example, that our health-care system is broken, yet they refuse to consider alternatives such as nationalized health care. If we just leave things alone, they reason, the system will fix itself.

Sometimes, conservatives' motivations for voting are questionable. Their basic rationale in the South, for instance, is revenge. Southerners switched to the Republican Party to exact revenge on the Democrats for passing civil rights laws that ended Jim Crow. As President Lyndon Johnson famously said following passage of the Civil Rights Act, "I think we just delivered the South to the Republican Party for a long time to come."[66] In the West, the federal government owns the majority of the land. People there tend to vote Republican, a party that supports states' rights.[67] This choice is in response to their sense of powerlessness, a theme that is also played out in their dreams. Neither desire for revenge nor a power play is a sign of a good mental attitude or example.

Fear of change is irrational. After all, the world has changed dramatically over thousands of years of recorded history. These people are also cowardly, as they are afraid to face the future. Conservatives admire the Founding Fathers immensely. Yet those people brought about great changes to society at great risk to their lives and fortunes. If you really admire someone, why not try to follow their example?

This fear is one reason why conservatives tend to have a higher voter turnout than liberals. Because they desperately want to prevent change, they make sure they show up at the polls in an effort to prevent it. Studies show that people will work twice as hard to avoid losing something as they will in trying to gain something.[68] Liberals, conversely, know that history is on their side and that change will eventually come, so they have no visceral motivation to spur them to the polls. Hence, liberal turnouts are often not as high. Presidential election results offer evidence for this dichotomy. Only three Democratic presidential candidates have received more than 55 percent of the popular vote (Jackson, Franklin Roosevelt [twice], and Lyndon Johnson). Eight Republicans have exceeded that figure (Lincoln, Grant, Theodore Roosevelt, Harding, Hoover, Eisenhower [twice], Nixon, and Reagan).[69]

History is progress. Consequently, by resisting progress, conservatives end up fighting history. It is always a losing battle. Why would anyone embrace a futile position that always puts them on the losing side?

One interesting phenomenon is how conservative talk radio draws a much larger audience than its liberal counterpart.[70] The reason for this has nothing to do with the skill of the hosts or quality of the programming, however. After all, if programming made a difference, liberals could simply copy the format and attract more listeners. Rather, this genre is successful because conservatives are in more need of reassurance. With change going on all around them, they need to tune in to someone who will tell them it is all right to resist change and maintain the status quo. Liberals, on the other hand, know they are on the right side of history and their view will ultimately prevail.[71]

Unfortunately, conservatives also have higher suicide rates. Ten states had rates of ten or fewer per one hundred thousand.[72] Of those, six are in the liberal Northeast: Maryland, New Jersey, New York, Massachusetts, Connecticut, and Rhode Island. Two are in the West: California and Hawaii. Illinois is the lone one in the Midwest. The only conservative state, and the only one in the South, is Georgia. Most of those with high rates are in the West, with Wyoming having the highest rate. Because conservatives fear change, some may see suicide as the only way out when their lives are overwhelmed by it. There is an interesting corollary to this finding. Other studies show that people who listen to country music are more likely to commit suicide.[73] Of course, this genre is most prevalent in the conservative South.

*Immorality*

Many Republicans tout their party as the champion of morality. Yet a close look at the record indicates otherwise. Following is a table of improprieties committed by governors and federal officials over the past three decades. Although not exhaustive, it is representative, having been culled from news reports of the time. Inclusion in the list is based on admission by the politician, proof in a court of law, or confirmation by investigative reporting. Mere allegations are not sufficient.

Some would argue that divorce should not be included. After all, it no longer prevents candidates from being elected to office. However, because some conservatives harp so much about all aspects of morality, it has been included. And it serves to reinforce the conclusion presented earlier, which is that conservatives are more likely to get divorced.

Conservatives may argue that the list is top-heavy with Republicans because they controlled the White House during the great majority of the time frame. However, the GOP controlled the House of Representatives for only twelve of those years, and they had a Senate majority for only sixteen years.[74] Moreover, Democrats controlled statehouses for sixteen of those years. Looking at the big picture, there are 535 members of Congress, but only fifty governors and a similar number in the White House. Therefore, the makeup of Congress, which was fairly even, reflects the overall distribution of power during this time.

This list is not intended to embarrass anyone or to criticize a particular party. Rather, it is presented to show that neither party has a claim on virtue or vice. To state otherwise is to ignore the facts.

**Political Improprieties**
**Divorce, Affairs, and Harassment**
**Financial and Other Scandals**
**Governors and Federal Officials**
**1981–2009**
*Republicans*
Ronald Reagan (Pres, D)
Bob Dole (S KS, D)
Phil Gramm (S TX, F)
Newt Gingrich (HR GA, D)
Pete Wilson (Gov CA, D)
Sonny Bono (HR CA, D)
Dan Burton (HR IN, A)
Helen Chenoweth (HR ID, D)
Arne Carlson (Gov MN, D)
Dick Armey (HR TX, D)
Bob Packwood (S OR, E)
Al D'Amato (S NY, D)
Henry Hyde (HR IL, A)
Jerry Weller (HR IL, D)
Enid Walpole (HR UT, D)
Rick White (HR WA, D)
J. C. Watts (HR OK, A)
Michael Huffington (HR CA, D)
Bob Livingston (HR LA, A)
Bob Barr (HR GA, D)
Kirk Fordice (Gov MS, D)

John McCain (S AZ, D)
John Porter (HR IL, D)
John Schmitz (HR CA, A)
Tim Hutchinson (S AR, D)
John Warner (S VA, D)
Oliver North (Iran Contra)
Adm. John Poindexter (Iran Contra)
Edwin Meese (AG, Iran Contra)
Lynn Nofziger (Press Secy, E)
Sam Pierce (HUD, E)
Evan Mecham (Gov AZ, F)
Fife Symington (Gov AZ, F)
Robin Carle (HR clerk)
James Watt (HUD scam)
Bud Shuster (HR PA, F/E)
Linda Chavez (E)
Elliott Abrams (Iran Contra)
Jane Swift (Gov MA, E)
Guy Hunt (Gov AL, F)
Richard Juliano (Bush admin, license for bribes)
Mike Huckabee (Gov AR, F)
John Snow (Treas Sec, F)
Bill Janklow (HR SD, manslaughter)
Strom Thurmond (S SC, A)
John Rowland (Gov CN, F)
John Hostettler (HR IN, illegal gun possession)
Tom Delay (HR TX, E)
Bob Taft (Gov OH, E)

Randy Cunningham (HR CA, F)
Bob Ney (HR OH, D)
Don Sherwood (HR PA, A)
George Ryan (Gov IL, F)
Mark Foley (HR FL, E)
Lester Crawford (EPA, E)
Mike Ferguson (HR NJ, E)
Steven Griles (Interior, E)
David Vitter (S LA, A)
Larry Craig (S ID, E)
Vito Fossella (HR NY, A)
Ted Stevens (S AK, F)
John Ensign (S NV, A)
Mark Sanford (Gov SC, A)
Mark Kirk (HR IL, D)

*Democrats*
Bill Clinton (Pres, A)
Ted Kennedy (S MA, D)
Charles Robb (Gov VA, A)
Mel Reynolds (HR IL, A)
Gary Hart (S CO, A)
Paul Patton (Gov KY, A)
Jim Wright (HR TX, E)
Web Hubbell (Asst AG, E)
Jim Guy Tucker (Gov AR, F)
Henry Cisneros (HUD, E)
Edwin Edwards (Gov LA, F)
Earl Hilliard (HR AL, F)

Dan Rostenkowski (HR IL, F)
James Traficant (HR OH, F)
Bob Wise (Gov WV, A)
Dennis Kucinich (HR OH, D)
John Kerry (S MA, D)
Charles Gonzelez (HR TX, D)
James McGreevey (Gov NJ, D/A)
Eliot Spitzer (Gov NY, A)
John Edwards (S NC, A)
William Jefferson (HR LA, F)

Key:

D = Divorce

A = Affair

F = Financial

E = Ethics

HR = House of Representatives

S = Senate

Gov = Governor

Pres = President

AG = Attorney General

Of greater concern is that merely exercising conservatism can push the limits of morality. For example, right-wingers may oppose progress because they are simply too lazy to make the necessary changes. Their arguments point to the difficulty of the undertaking. For example, some claim that preventing global warming would require us to make major lifestyle changes.[75] However, many accomplishments in life take considerable effort, so this is a specious argument at best.

Another problem with conservatism is that it can be used as an excuse for revenge. As discussed previously, conservative Southerners left the Democratic Party and began to vote Republican because they opposed the civil rights laws. Using political views to punish people is certainly not a good example, to say the least.

Conservatives tend to overlook sins of omission. For example, they are often quick to point the finger at people who commit wrongful acts. When liberals point out that failing to help the poor is also wrong, some conservatives say they do not engage in "moral equivalency."[76] But God does, of course. Conservatives fail to realize that Sodom and Gomorrah were destroyed because they neglected the poor.[77] When it comes to right and wrong, it is important to look not only at what we do but also at what we fail to do.

Because the logic of conservatism is flawed, they often resort to distortion of the truth to defend their positions. Sometimes, this results in outright lies. House Minority Leader John Boehner, for instance, said Obama's proposed health-care reform plan would force seniors to submit to euthanasia. In reality, it only agreed to pay for voluntary end-of-life counseling.[78] Unfortunately, lies are the last refuge of the desperate.

Another favorite conservative strategy is the "red herring," something that draws attention from the issue at hand. A good example is when they propose limiting medical malpractice awards as the solution to high health-care costs. Because caps would save only $5.4 billion a year[79] in a $2.5 trillion system, the impact of such a change is marginal. The intended effect, of course, is to distract people from the need for major health-care reform.

More often, though, conservatives resort to slanting the truth. One way of doing this is to ignore facts that would blow apart their arguments. Another is to make blanket statements. A favorite charge of the political right is to claim that all programs run by the government are a mess. This, of course, is a gross generalization. Most seniors, for example, are pleased with Medicare. And the National Institutes of Health (NIH) have done much to make our lives safer and better. Among NIH successes is a test for human immunodeficiency virus (HIV). The return on their research is estimated to be 25 to 40 percent. And of the twenty-one drugs introduced from 1965–1992 that had the highest therapeutic value, public funding was instrumental in fifteen.[80]

Believe it or not, the Internet is also a product of the government. To be precise, it involved several governments. Fermilab in Batavia, Illinois, was in on the ground floor, as the Internet was originally developed to exchange scientific information. Scientists there primarily credit two people. In this country, Senator Al Gore sponsored the bill establishing the department in the National Science Foundation that set up the Internet. Timothy Berners-Lee, a British computer programmer working at the European Center for Nuclear Research in Geneva, Switzerland, developed the World Wide Web.[81] Of course, the Internet has since evolved to include information from many different areas, not just science.[82]

One purported liberal failure, public housing, deserves a closer look. This program actually succeeded in New York City, but it failed in Chicago and Los Angeles.[83] Naturally, New Yorkers insist that was because they managed it better. However, the real reason was because New York had an advantage over the other two cities. It is very compact (based on population density)[84] and has an excellent public transportation system. As a result, people living in public housing could easily commute to their jobs. Chicago is more spread out and offers less in the way of public transportation. Los Angeles is even more spread out with very little mass transit. Because people in the latter two cities could not easily get to where the jobs were, poverty persisted in the public housing units. The program failed due to infrastructure shortcomings in Chicago and Los Angeles, not because public housing was a bad idea or New Yorkers were smarter. Having learned this lesson, the Chicago Housing Authority is now moving people from the housing projects to subsidized apartments throughout the city.[85]

If the old way is really best, as conservatives claim, then why not take that view to its logical conclusion? We should be riding around on horseback, living in caves, and being subject to monarchs. The reality, of course, is that conservatives can accept the world they are born into, but they do not want it to change during their lifetimes. Such an attitude seems incredibly selfish. If we see a way to make the world a better place, we should do so.

# Chapter 6
# The Future

Looking at conservatism from different perspectives reveals its shortcomings. Historically, the data trends show that it achieves nothing of lasting value. Liberal accomplishments, on the other hand, live on for many generations. Economically, conservatism causes major recessions through its penchant for deregulation. Consequently, the economy is stronger under liberal leaders. Socially, conservatism prevents a just society by acting out of fear. Politically, conservatism, by definition, stands in the way of progress by fighting change. Having considered this comparison, what should our response be?

At this point, some might be tempted to say that political moderates incorporate the best of both worlds. However, a moderate is someone who is willing to take one step forward when two are required. A case in point is the health-care issue. Both sides agree the system is a mess; only major surgery will do.

Libertarians also seem to think they have the best of both worlds, although they come at it from a different angle. The crux of their belief is that government involvement in our lives should be no more than absolutely necessary. As a result, they tend to be social liberals and economic conservatives. In the latter view, they tend to espouse an unfettered free market.[86] Of course, the recent recession shot that approach down.

Conservatism and liberalism are opposing views; both cannot be right. Either change is bad, and this is the best we can do, or we can find ways to make the world a better place. Clearly, the foregoing discussion shows that no case can be made for conservatism in any area: social, political, historical, or economic.

Independents, who are more likely to change their minds and seem to believe that both sides have something to offer, lead the political cycle. Yet nothing could be further from the truth.

If we really want to end major economic dislocations, then voting for conservatives is not the answer. Their worship of the free market is a fatal flaw in their philosophy. The majority of people have taken two big hits to their stock portfolios over the past decade. If we are to save enough for retirement, we must maintain a government that is friendly to the markets. Historically, that has been the Democratic Party.

The goal, therefore, is to eliminate the conservative part of the historical cycle. This will take a conscious effort, of course. However, the benefits will be great. Major recessions will finally become a thing of the past, for one thing. Moreover, society will advance at a more rapid pace, making our lives better. And programs that lead to an increase in crime, such as Prohibition and the war on drugs,[87] will no longer be adopted.

Some would lament this as the end of the two-party system. Perhaps, but it is important to remember that liberals do not agree on every issue. Afghanistan and health care are two recent examples of their differences. Most importantly, though, this change would force voters to focus on the candidates, which they should have been doing all along.

Even conservatives sometimes acknowledge the need for liberal solutions. Just as there are no atheists in a foxhole, so there are no conservatives in a crisis. Big business came running to the government for a bailout during the recent financial meltdown. When BP's oil spill threatened Louisiana's shoreline, its Republican governor looked to Washington for help. It is easy to embrace a belief when it is purely theoretical. Once it is put to the test, however, actions speak louder than words.

Military leaders know that fortune favors the bold. Admiral Farragut said, "Damn the torpedoes. Full speed ahead." Lord Cardigan commanded, "Forward the Light Brigade." And Captain Kirk ordered, "Ahead Warp 5, Mr. Sulu." Falling back into the old way will not lead to lasting success. Only bold action will result in progress toward a better world.

Well, this book has finally come to an end. After reading it, I hope you have decided to take the same journey I did, from conservatism to liberalism, based on rational thought. Here's to the future!

# Appendix

This book was written for the general public. As such, it does not go into great detail in certain areas, such as economics. For the more serious reader, the following discussion will help fill in that information.

The prevailing view is that energy price spikes caused the mid-1970s recession by reducing consumption. However, a study[88] showed that consumer purchases actually increased slightly during the downturn. On the other hand, investments declined by $89 billion. Because inflation was high, there was no rise in real interest rates in spite of the Fed increase. The author concludes that the decline in investment came from the expectation that the economy was going to be put through even higher interest rates to reduce inflation.

The consensus is that double-digit inflation was finally subdued by Fed rate increases that led to the early 1980s recession. A careful reader will have noticed that I disagree with this view. As I stated, the causes of inflation—energy price hikes and baby boomers' influx into the housing market—were beyond the Fed's ability to control with interest rates. Both causes came to an end in the early 1980s. There was no impact from the Fed, which had actually ratcheted up rates a few years earlier. Of course, politicians are loath to admit to the voters that anything is beyond their control, so they instead saddle us with multiple recessions.

\*\*\*

Undoubtedly, some conservatives will claim that certain events, such as the end of the Cold War, should be included in the table in chapter 1. They believe Reagan's massive defense buildup forced the Soviets to do the same, which ultimately proved unsustainable. A Central Intelligence Agency (CIA) report,[89] however, dispels this notion. Its conclusion was that the Union of Soviet Socialist Republics (USSR) could continue high levels of military spending for years to come. Political and economic deterioration caused the breakup of the Soviet Union and the end of the Cold War. Moreover, China had begun market reforms in the 1970s, so the Cold War was already winding down long before Reagan ever took office. It should also be noted that this event did not have the same impact on American society as did the others in the list. Indeed, most of the effect was felt in the former Soviet republics. So this item was excluded for good reason.

\*\*\*

It has been mentioned that some conservatives have become liberals because of events in their lives. Of course, conservatives would point out that liberals have also switched sides. True, but opposing change because of failure only means that they will never have a chance at success.

***

The higher marriage rate in the South is one additional variable that could affect the higher divorce rate (per one thousand population). To examine this possibility, I divided the divorce rate (per one thousand population) by the marriage rate[90] (per one thousand population) to yield the percentage of marriages that end in divorce. For eight of eleven Southern states for which this data was available, the percentage was higher than the national average. Therefore, higher marriage rates in the South do not account for the higher divorce rate.

New York did not adopt a no-fault divorce law until 2010, so no subsequent data is available for purposes of comparison. However, both Ohio and Michigan have poverty rates similar to Oklahoma, Alabama, Arkansas, and Tennessee.[91] Yet Ohio and Michigan also have divorce rates below the national average, so poverty does not account for regional differences in the divorce rate.

***

The items in the table in chapter 1 were major social, political, and economic events taken from a summary of American history in the *World Almanac*. They were then slotted into historical periods based on a best fit of the data. Certainly additional items could be included here. However, they would still follow the same trend. Events in each cycle would exhibit the traits of the dominant political philosophy in that cycle. Progress and reform mark the liberal eras, while resistance to both change and governmental regulation characterize the conservative times. Liberal changes continue even through subsequent conservative periods, while events in the conservative years come to an end during those years. Technological achievements and foreign affairs were excluded for reasons previously discussed (i.e., the former do not follow the historical trend, while the latter do not significantly affect American society).

The names and incidents in the table in chapter 5 were collected in real time, not through traditional research into past events. Those who desire more information can search the listed individuals.

*** 

The reference that discussed conservative traits[92] is interesting, although it is somewhat technical in nature. Its authors performed a linear regression on the data and then reported the correlation coefficients for each factor. Listed in descending order, the variables for conservatism are death anxiety, system instability, intolerance of ambiguity, need for order, and fear of threat and loss. Those with negative coefficients are liberal traits. These are openness to experience, uncertainty tolerance, integrative complexity, and self-esteem (also listed in descending order). Fear is identified as an external stimulus of political conservatism. The two core dimensions of conservative thought are resistance to change and endorsement of inequality.

***

The article on talk radio considered two possible causes for the disparity. Some have attributed the dominance of conservative talk radio to the repeal of the Fairness Doctrine by the Federal Communications Commission in 1987. At any rate, the Fairness Doctrine was never actually repealed, so this argument is not valid. Others argue that stations are merely responding to market forces. Yet the ratio of conservative to liberal radio listeners is far less than the 91 percent of programming that is conservative, so, in the authors' view, this is not a good explanation either. They then posit that structural problems are the cause. Specifically, they believe there are not enough female- and minority-owned stations that would be more likely to air liberal programs. Given that conservative radio listeners outnumber liberals by nearly two-to-one, boosting ownership beyond the white males who dominate the medium would likely not overcome the huge advantage of conservative programming. Moreover, it is implausible that owners would jeopardize profits by ignoring market forces. This leaves the audience itself as the only factor that explains the difference. Conservatives simply have a much greater inherent need for this format.

\*\*\*

For purposes of analysis, recessions that were longer than six months and had peak unemployment rates greater than 6 percent were considered major. Durations[93] and unemployment rates[94] were obtained from published data. The 1937 recession was deemed to be a double-dip of the Great Depression and was not included.

\*\*\*

Early in World War II, Hitler prohibited research on any weapons that took more than a year to develop, since he believed the war would be over quickly.[95] This policy prevented Germany from many technological breakthroughs, including the atomic bomb. They did produce jet fighter airplanes, but only because Messerschmitt did the work in secret against Hitler's orders for a bomber.[96] Unfortunately for Germany, the fighter did not take to the skies in large numbers until the closing weeks of the war, making it too little, too late.

Most companies cut research spending during a recession, since the payout is long-term. After the dotcom bubble burst in 2000, Steve Jobs went against the grain by increasing Apple's research and development. He hoped to invent many new products that would put the company ahead of its competitors. As a result, the iPod, the iTunes store, Apple stores, and a new operating system all came out of the downturn. Today Apple is the world's most valuable company.[97]

In war and in peace, it pays to always be finding a better way of doing things. This principle also applies in the social, political, and economic realms. If we fail to find a better way, we will be condemned to repeat the mistakes of the past.

\*\*\*

Some would argue that the ratio of presidents with at least 55 percent of the popular vote is skewed, since the two parties had different ideologies in the nineteenth century (i.e., Democrats were conservative, while Republicans were liberal). However,

Lincoln's margin was tainted, since the South did not vote in that election. After eliminating that data point and switching Jackson and Grant, the conservative to liberal ratio becomes seven-to-three. That is similar to the eight-to-three ratio that was presented previously.

# References

1. James Hohmann, "On anniversary, Jim Brady continues gun-control push," *Politico*, 30 Mar. 2011.
2. "Reshaping of the Political Environment in Montana: Implications for Montana Fish, Wildlife and Parks," Montana Fish, Wildlife & Parks, 2004.
3. Arthur M. Schlesinger, Jr., *The Cycles of American History* (Houghton Mifflin, 1986).
4. *Time*, 15 Nov. 1968.
5. Kate Cruikshank, *The Art of Leadership: A Companion to an Exhibition of the Senatorial Papers of Birch Bayh, United States Senator from Indiana, 1963–1980* (The Trustees of Indiana University, 2010).
6. *World Almanac* (Pleasantville: World Almanac Books, 2012), 450.
7. Pat Buchanan, "Newspaper: Butterfly Ballot Cost Gore White House," *CNN Politics*, 11 Mar. 2001.
8. *World Almanac* (Pleasantville: World Almanac Books, 2012), 456.
9. "No Child Left Behind," *Education Week*, 4 Aug. 2004.
10. Kristi Keck, "Divided Democrats put Obama in health care bind," *CNN Politics*, 21 Aug. 2009.

11. Rachel Sklar, "Remnick On Clinton On Everything, Picked Up By Nothing," *The Huffington Post*, 18 Sept. 2006.
12. "Bush got bum rap for Sosa deal," *The Washington Times*, 27 July 2005.
13. Tim Weiner, "Robert S. McNamara, Architect of a Futile War, Dies at 93," *New York Times*, 6 July 2009.
14. Carroll Kilpatrick, "Nixon Tells Editors, 'I'm Not a Crook,'" *Washington Post*, 18 Nov. 1973.
15. Brian Williams, "The 11th Commandment," *The Daily Nightly on NBC News*, 17 Oct. 2007.
16. Arthur A. Sloane, *Hoffa* (MIT Press, 1991); Damon Stetson, "Brennan Reports Labor Leaders Favoring Nixon Are Organizing," *New York Times*, 9 Sept. 1972.
17. Christopher B. Kenney, Michael McBurnett, and David J. Bordua, *Does the National Rifle Association Affect Federal Elections?* (Independence Institute, 2006).
18. Andrew Sullivan, "The Emptiness of Karl Rove," *The Atlantic*, 27 Nov. 2009.
19. Paul Krugman, May 14, 2003, *PBS News Hour.*
20. "List of recessions in the United States," *Wikipedia*, 14 June 2012.
21. Bob DeMaura, "Barack and the Democrats Caused the Recession!" *NH Insider*, 15 June 2012.
22. *New York Times*, 4 Nov. 1992.
23. See note 22 above.
24. "The Prospects for Economic Recovery," Congressional Budget Office, Feb. 1982.
25. Jim Lehrer, Sept. 18, 2007, *PBS News Hour.*
26. Naomi Klein, "Alan Greenspan and the Myth of the True Believer," *The Nation*, 28 Sept. 2007.
27. *Chicago Tribune*, 23 Dec. 2001, business section.
28. Robert Bryce, "From Enron to the Financial Crisis, With Alan Greenspan in Between," *U. S. News & World Report*, 24 Sept. 2008.

29. David Weisberg, "What Caused the Great Recession?" *Newsweek Magazine*, 8 Jan. 2010.
30. Edmund L. Andrews, "Greenspan Concedes Error on Regulation," *New York Times*, 23 Oct. 2008.
31. Dan Barufaldi, "A Review of Past Recessions," *Investopedia* (2010).
32. James L. Williams, "Market Share within OPEC," *WTRG Economics* (1999).
33. George F. Will, "Economically, Obama May Repeat FDR's Mistakes," *Washington Post*, 30 Nov. 2008.
34. Peter Baker, "Bill Clinton's Legacy," *Washington Post*, 3 Feb. 2008.
35. Stephen Labaton, "Agency's '04 Rule Lets Banks Pile Up New Debt," *New York Times*, 7 Oct. 2008.
36. Kemper Funds newsletter (Winter/Spring 1998).
37. Daniel Kadlec, "Vote for Gridlock," *Time*, 28 Aug. 2000, 66.
38. Edmund L. Andrews and Graham Bowley, "Dow Rises 370 Points as U. S. Plans Financial Rescue Package," *New York Times*, 19 Sept. 2008.
39. Janet Kidd Stewart, "Voters Take Stock of Candidates' Ideas for the Economy," *Chicago Tribune*, 3 Sept. 2000, section 5, page 6.
40. William Roscoe Thayer, *Theodore Roosevelt: An Intimate Biography* (1919), Chapter XXII, 25–31.
41. David Silbey, "The Ghost at the (Democratic) Banquet," *The Chronicle of Higher Education*, 28 Apr. 2009.
42. *Chicago Tribune*, 28 Jan. 2000.
43. Pew Research Center, "Public Praises Science; Scientists Fault Public, Media," *Scientists, Politics and Religion*, 9 July 2009, section 4.
44. *Time*, 20 May 2002 ; *Chicago Tribune*, 4 Oct. 2003.
45. *Chicago Tribune Magazine*, 21 Dec. 2003.

46. Annette Cox, "Textiles: The Textile Industry in the United States," *The Oxford Encyclopedia of the Modern World, Vol. 7* (2008), 244.

47. John T. Jost, Jack Glaser, Arie W. Kruglanski, and Frank J. Sulloway, "Political Conservatism as Motivated Social Cognition," *Psychological Bulletin*, 2003, Vol. 129, No. 3, 339–375.

48. See note 47 above.

49. See note 47 above.

50. Kelly Bulkeley, PhD, Conference of the Association for the Study of Dreams, July 2001.

51. David Crary, "Bible Belt is also Divorce Belt," *Chicago Tribune*, 12 Nov. 1999.

52. Dennis A. Ahlburg and Carol J. De Vita, "New Realities of the American Family," Population Bulletin (August 1992).

53. *World Almanac* (Pleasantville: World Almanac Books, 2009), 89.

54. Belinda Luscombe, "Divorcing by the Numbers," *Time*, 24 May 2010, 47.

55. J. B. Judis and R. Teixeira, "Back to the Future," *The American Prospect*, 19 June 2007.

56. Michael Barbaro, "Bush's Daughter, in a Break, Endorses Gay Marriage," *New York Times*, 31 Jan. 2011.

57. Jason Leopold, "Cheney Admits He 'Signed Off' on Waterboarding of Three Guantanamo Prisoners," *Atlantic Free Press*, 29 Dec. 2008.

58. John G. Hubbell, *P. O. W.: A Definitive History of the American Prisoner-of-War Experience in Vietnam, 1964–1973* (New York: Reader's Digest Press, 1976), 363.

59. See note 56 above.

60. MSN Encarta, "George Bush" (Microsoft, 2009).

61. Baseball-Reference.com, Texas Rangers: Team History & Encyclopedia (Sports Reference LLC, 2000–2012).

62. Bonnie Miller Robin, "Is Workplace Better If She's the Boss?" *Chicago Tribune*, 9 Aug. 2003.

63. Janet Kidd Steward and T. Shawn Taylor, "Lightning Layoffs May Not Pay Off," *Chicago Tribune*, 1 May 2001.

64. Megan McArdle, "Why Companies Fail," *Atlantic Magazine*, Mar. 2012.

65. Timothy Curry and Lynn Shibut, "The Cost of the Savings and Loan Crisis: Truth and Consequences," *FDIC Banking Review*, Dec. 2000, 26–34.

66. "Second Thoughts: Reflections on the Great Society," *New Perspectives Quarterly* (Winter 1987).

67. See note 41 above.

68. David Kahneman and Amos Tversky, "Prospect Theory: An Analysis of Decision under Risk," *Econometrica* 47 (1979), 263–291.

69. David Leip, *Dave Leip's Atlas of U. S. Presidential Elections*.

70. John Halpin, James Heidbreder, Mark Lloyd, Paul Woodhull, Ben Scott, Josh Silver, and S. Derek Turner, "The Structural Imbalance of Political Talk Radio," *Center for American Progress*, 20 June 2007.

71. Daniel Shea, "Letter: why I am a liberal, a response," *The Huntington News*, 19 Apr. 2012.

72. Colleen Mastony, "Young Man's Fatal Leap Haunts Witnesses," *Chicago Tribune*, 15 Nov. 2009.

73. S. Stack and J. H. Gundlach, "The Effects of Country Music on Suicide," *Social Forces* 71 (1) (1992), 211–218.

74. *World Almanac* (Pleasantville: World Almanac Books, 2009), 446.

75. Faiz Shakir, "'Smokey Joe' Barton: Global Warming 'Is A Net Benefit to Mankind,'" *Think Progress*, 14 Dec. 2009.

76. Christian Heinze, "Christians, Abortion, Iowa, and Rights," *The Hill*, 26 Apr. 2009.

77. Ezekiel 16:49.

78. Carrie Budoff Brown, "Will Proposal Promote Euthanasia?" *Politico*, 28 July 2009.

79. Noam N. Levey, "Tough Choices on Health Care: Numerous Issues Could Derail Bill in Senate," *Chicago Tribune*, 24 Nov. 2009.
80. Joint Economic Committee of Congress, 2000.
81. Dr. Chuck Brown, Fermilab Presentation to American Institute of Chemical Engineers Chicago Section, 10 May 2006.
82. *World Almanac* (Pleasantville: World Almanac Books, 2012), 364.
83. James Hanlon, "The Perseverance of Public Housing in New York City," H-Net: Humanities & Social Sciences Online, Sept. 2008.
84. *World Almanac* (Pleasantville: World Almanac Books, 2009), 552.
85. "Scattered Site Properties," Chicago Housing Authority.
86. Libertarian Party Platform, Libertarian Party website, adopted May 2012.
87. Linnet Myers, "Europe Finds U. S. Drug War Lacking in Results," *Chicago Tribune*, 2 Nov. 1992, pp. 1, 24–25.
88. Thayer Watkins, "The Recession of 1973–75 in the U. S.," San Jose State University: Department of Economics.
89. Michael Kilian, "Gorbachev's Failures with Economy Ended Cold War, CIA Reports," *Chicago Tribune*, 19 Nov. 1999, 22.
90. *Statistical Abstract of the United States* (U. S. Census Bureau, 2012). Table 133. Marriages and Divorces— Number and Rate by State: 1990–2009.
91. See note 53 above.
92. See note 47 above.
93. "NBER Business Cycle Expansions and Contractions," National Bureau of Economic Research.
94. "Labor Force Statistics from the Current Population Survey," Bureau of Labor Statistics.
95. "Hitler's Ten Biggest Strategic Mistakes," *World Defence*, 2010.

96. Alfred Price, *The Last Year of the Luftwaffe: May 1944 to May 1945* (London: Greenhill Books, 1993), 176.
97. Rana Faroohar, "What Would Steve Do?" *Time*, 27 Feb. 2012, 18.

# NOTES

# NOTES

# NOTES

# About the author

Stephen Schade is a chemical engineer with a master's degree in chemical engineering from the University of Missouri–Rolla (now Missouri University of Science and Technology). He grew up in Cape Girardeau, Missouri, and currently lives in Mount Prospect, Illinois.